There are five titles in the 'Get Going With Creative Writing' series:

All About Me – 978-1-907733-90-1

Likes and Dislikes – 978-1-907733-91-8

Out and About – 978-1-907733-92-5

We Love Animals – 978-1-907733-93-2

What We Do – 978-1-907733-94-9

Guinea Pig Education
2 Cobs Way
New Haw, Addlestone
Surrey
KT15 3AF
Tel: 01932 336553
Website: www.guineapigeducation.co.uk

© Copyright 2014

NO part of this publication may be reproduced, stored or copied for commercial purposes and profit without the prior written permission of the publishers.

ISBN: 978-1-907733-93-2

Written: Sally A Jones and Amanda C Jones
Illustrations: Sally A Jones
Graphic Design: Annalisa Jones
USA Editing: S. Waller

Dear Kids,

Have fun learning to write with our 'Get Going With Creative Writing' series. Enjoy reading our short stories; some of which have been written by kids your age. Use our ideas to write your own stories, or try some non-fiction writing, such as, diaries, reports and leaflets. If you read or write well you will achieve high grades at school, so we challenge you to learn to love writing. You just need a notebook and pencil to start working through your guinea pig writing guide. Don't forget to color in the pictures.

Dear Teachers and Parents,

If your children think writing is dull, give them a guinea pig writing book from the 'Get Going With Creative Writing' series and we think they'll change their minds. However, these books are also ideal for those children who love to write, providing starting points that will make any budding young writer's imagination run wild, especially if they are preparing for standardized tests.

We have put together a series of themed books to inspire your child to write at his or her level. Whether you choose 'About Me,' 'We Love Animals,' 'Likes and Dislikes,' 'Out And About' or 'What We Do,' you will choose an English study book with a light-hearted, modern approach to appeal to the children of today.

The books can be used at home or in school alongside the existing curriculum. Inside, you will find a treasure trove of ideas for writing, featuring fiction and non-fiction themes. Based on the National Curriculum in the UK, they use respected strategies for literacy, with tips on planning and writing techniques, sentence construction, grammar tips and more.

Written by a former teacher, working as a tutor, the books have been tested by the children the author teaches in Surrey, England. These children agree the books are fun and help them learn to love writing.

> **We would like to thank the students of Guinea Pig Tuition – class of 2010/2011 – Sophia, Georgina, Harriet, Hannah, Sacha, Harry, Gareth, Rahan, Neena, Mahir, Neesha, Jai, Alexandra, Anna Maria and Vlad.**

Let's **meet** Hugo.

I am a cute, cuddly and adorable creature that lives in a cage in the garden: perhaps I live in a cage in your garden.

Let's write.

Answer each question in a sentence. Don't forget to start each sentence with a capital letter and end with a period.

- What do I **look** *like*?

- What is my **character** *like*?

- What do I **think about** as I *sit* in my *cage*?

Finish the sentences by choosing one of the endings.

Hugo has an **adventure**.

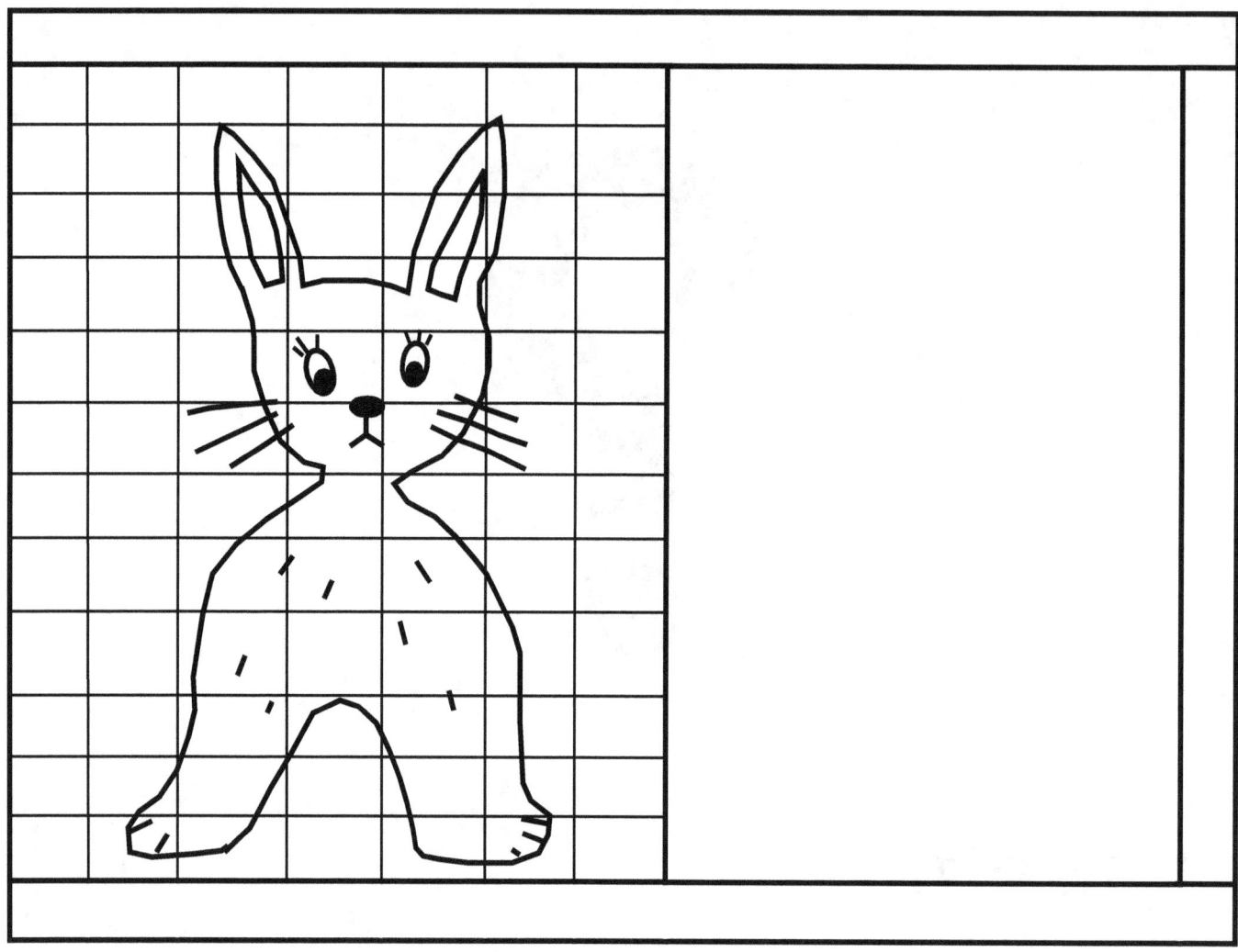

Paragraph 1

One morning, I sat in my hutch staring at the …

- delicious dandelion leaves.
- busy bees.
- active ants.
- scuttling spiders.
- green grass.
- ……………………………………

Cramped up in my cage, I felt bored because…

- *I had nothing to do.*
- *I wanted to eat the fresh leaves.*
- *I needed to exercise my paws.*
- *I could not run and jump on the lawn.*
- *the scent of new grass made me want to play outside.*

Playfully, I pushed on the door of my cage with my strong legs, until it made a …

- *creaking sound.*
- *cracking sound.*
- *splintering sound.*

The lock, that was not fixed securely, snapped open with a …

- *thud.*
- *bang.*
- *crash.*

Then I hopped down onto the green grass …
- *full of joy.*
- *twitching my nose.*
- *casting a sideways glance at the house.*
- ....

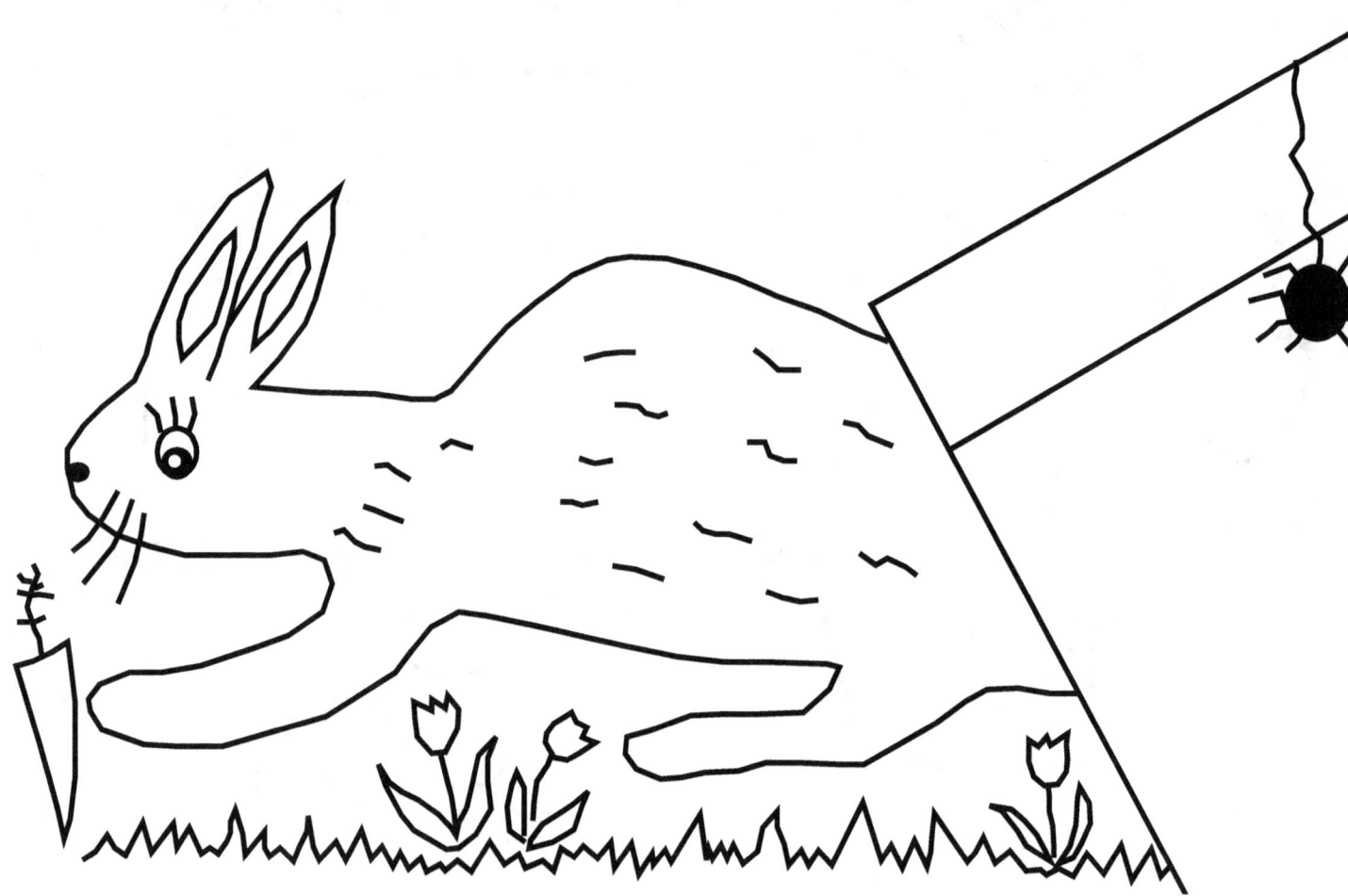

Paragraph 2

First, I nibbled greedily at the …
- *tender shoots.*
- *lovely leaves.*
- *tasty buds.*
- ....

After this, I raced around the garden ...

- *leaping in the air.*
- *chewing through flower heads.*
- *catching gnats in the air.*
- ....

Feeling tired, I decided to make a new place to hide, so I ...

- *scrabbled with my paws in the flowerbed.*
- *started to tunnel under the shed.*
- *dug a deep channel through the lawn.*
- ....

As I was about to flop down to rest, I heard the door open. Then a human voice ....

- *screamed loudly.*
- *shouted at the top of her voice.*
- *yelled frantically.*

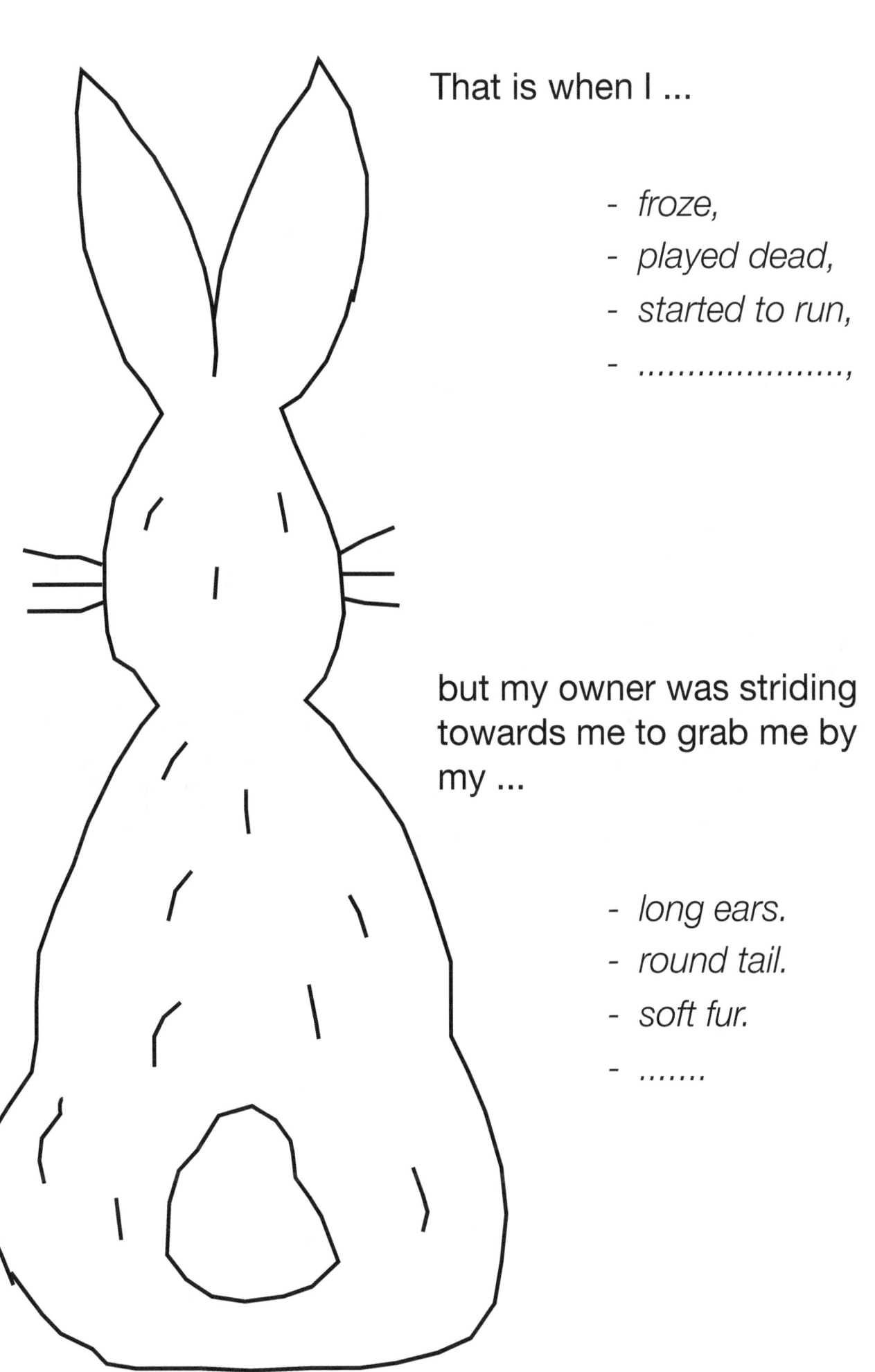

That is when I ...

- *froze,*
- *played dead,*
- *started to run,*
- *....................,*

but my owner was striding towards me to grab me by my ...

- *long ears.*
- *round tail.*
- *soft fur.*
- *.......*

Paragraph 3

Then I scampered like an athlete; I ran as fast as my legs would carry me ...

- *through the door of the house.*
- *under the shed.*
- *around the garden table.*

Soon, I was so out of breath that I...

- *skidded to a halt.*
- *ran into the fence with a bang.*
- *collapsed on the compost heap.*
- *got stuck in a hole.*
- ....

Then the warm hand of my owner ...

- *grabbed me.*
- *seized hold of me.*
- *picked me up.*
- *...................*

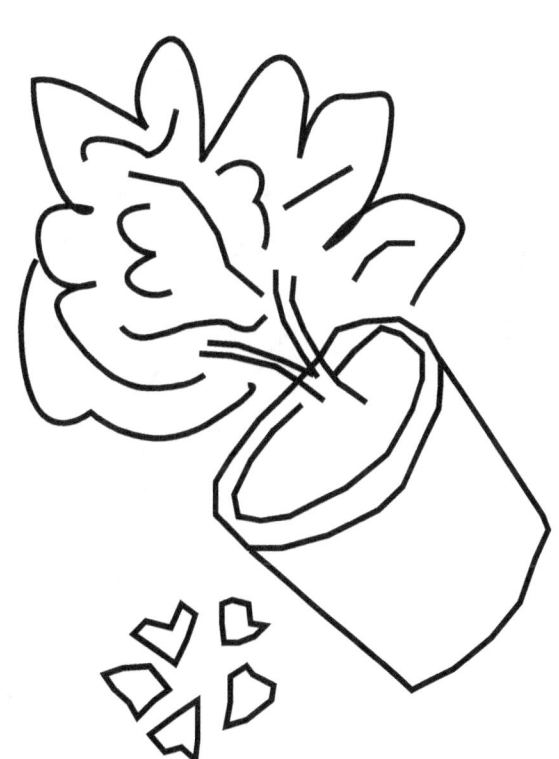

In protest ...

- *I scratched,*
- *I bit,*
- *I struggled,*

... but it was too late; I was caught.

Later, I was so pleased because...
- *I was sprawled out comfortably on the sofa.*
- *my owner was stroking me gently.*
- *I was bedded down in clean straw.*

Choose one of the endings on this page.

Later, I was feeling disgruntled because ...
- *I had missed my dinner.*
- *my owner was angry with me.*
- *I had no cuddles today.*
- *..*

Plan your *own* **animal story**.

Think about an animal like Hugo and answer these questions.

1. What does he **look like**?

Write about:
- *his pointed ears*
- *his brown eyes*
- *his strong black legs*
- *his wet nose*
- *his soft fur*
- ....

2. What is his **character like**?

Write about:
- how gentle and kind he is.
- how he likes to be stroked.
- how clumsy he is when he knocks over his food bowl.
- how naughty he is when he escapes from his cage.
- ....

Now answer these questions.

3. What does he **think about** as he **sits** in his **cage**?

4. What does he **see**?

5. Has somebody **left** the cage door **open**?

6. What is he **thinking** now?

7. How does he **get out** of his cage?

8. **Where** does he **go**?

9. **What** does he **do**?

10. "**My rabbit has escaped!**" How does the owner feel?

11. Is there a **big chase**?

12. Does he **run around** the **garden**?

13. Does **something get broken**?

14. How does he **get caught**?

15. **What** does his owner **say** and **do**?

16. Is he soon **forgiven**?

17. **Back in his hutch** or cage, **how** does your **animal feel** now?

Use your answers to write a story in three paragraphs.

What does my rabbit look like?

My little bunny rabbit called Hugo is handsome. He has long, pointed ears and big, brown eyes that stare lovingly at me. His legs are strong, so I have to be careful he doesn't kick me when I lift him out of his cage. Hugo has such soft fur that I stroke, stroke and stroke him.

What is his character like?

Hugo behaves like a prince. When I bring him inside the house, he stretches himself out regally on the sofa. Even if he is hungry, he is always gentle, but he is a very greedy animal and gobbles his food down quickly. Sometimes he even knocks his food bowl over, spilling food on the floor. Then he'll have a naughty moment and race around the house, knocking things over.

What does he like to do?

Best of all, he likes to be brushed, stroked and tickled under his ears. He likes to cuddle up in the warm straw in his hutch. Then he likes to sit in his run and watch insects on the grass. However, on fine days he likes to escape, so he can eat the plants in our garden.

Use the headings to write about a pet.

Time to tune into Guinea Pig FM RADIO

Listen Live

Hi, I'm your D.J. George:

... and I'm Christabelle:

How are you today?

I'm good. How about you?

Well, I've had a bad day...

How come?

It's that new guinea pig. You know… I let him run around my apartment. I didn't think he could come to any harm, but he's gone and chewed through the T.V. cable with his sharp teeth.

No! That's really dangerous.

He's cost me a lot of money. I've had to call an electrician and he can't come till Thursday, so I'm without a T.V.

Oh no! That's awful!

Today I want the listeners to send in their **animal horror stories**. Think of a time when your animal did something really bad. Contact us now by text, phone or email…

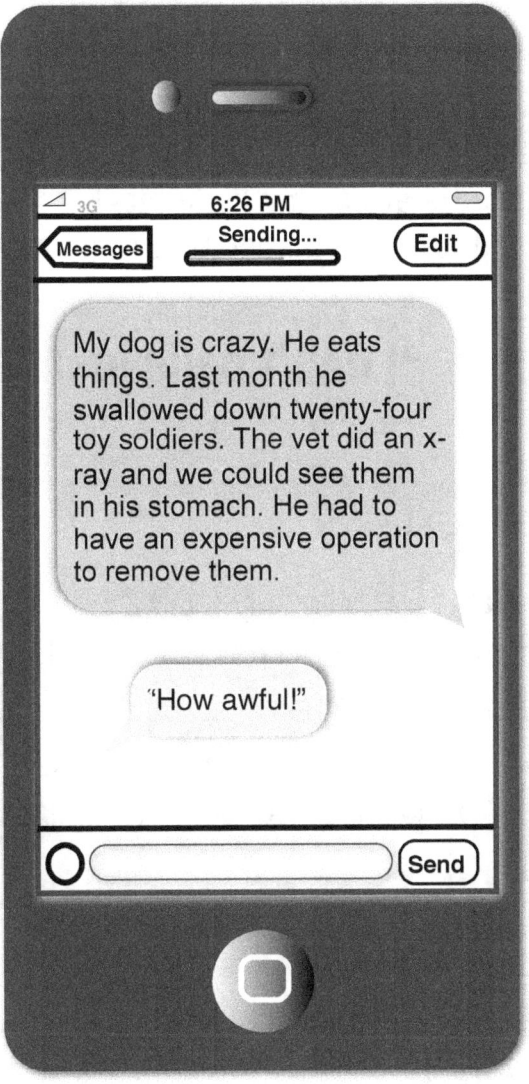

Sam writes…

Walking my dog is a nightmare. Last week my dog raced off in the park. He got into a fight. He barked and growled at other dogs. Then he ran off through a hole in the fence and got home before me.

Candice texts…

```
If my dog sees a
cat, he's off! If
I'm walking him
on his leash he
pulls me along.
```

"Oh no!"

"We have Leanne on the line.

Hello Leanne. What is your story?"

"Well, George, there was a scary noise in our house. It was a tapping sound: everyday it got louder and louder. We thought it was a ghost. We investigated the place where the noise was coming from; it was under the stairs. A builder came to investigate. He opened up the banister. We got the shock of our lives! Out popped a pointed face and whiskers… It was our neighbor's missing hamster."

"Wow! What a story."

Can you write one?

RABBITS! My garden is trashed! They snapped off the heads of all my lovely flowers. They've eaten all the plants… so it's just thick mud. Now they just dig, dig, dig all day– my garden looks like a playground.

	New	Reply	Reply all	Foward	Delete	Mark as ▼	Move to ▼

INBOX (240)

FOLDERS

Junk (109)

Drafts (11)

Sent

Deleted (15)

New Folder

Animal Horror Stories

☐ **D.J. George** 09/11/2014
To George@guineapig.co.uk **Reply**

My cat went fishing in my neighbor's pond and caught one of his huge prize winning fish. They were his pride and joy. My cat put it on the patio and proceeded to have a feast. He ate every little bit. I don't dare to tell my neighbor. He would have been absolutely furious!

Harry

"I can't believe it."

Kirsty writes…

My dog growled at a waiter in a restaurant. Then he grabbed his tie with his teeth and held onto it.

"Yuck! That's disgusting."

Laura texts…

My friend's cat brought in a mouse through the window… Guess what? It was still in a trap!

Cody texts…

```
My cat brings in mice and we chase
them around the room. He also brings
in birds and frogs. Sometimes the
house is chaos, with creatures
flying and hopping around crazily!
```

Write these stories in three paragraphs.

James texts…

```
My cat went up the
chimney and got stuck
trying to get a bird,
so we had to call the
fire department to free
him.
```

Let's end on a sad one.
Ella writes…

My rabbit and guinea pig mysteriously disappeared from my back garden one evening. We searched and searched, but never found them. I think they were stolen.

"These stories just get more and more hilarious!"

My cat is:

affectionate	agile	naughty	mischievous
lazy	powerful	sweet natured	devoted
friendly	fast	playful	cute
cuddly	sly	intelligent	loyal
sensitive	sneaky	stubborn	proud
energetic	smart	home loving	clever
independent	defiant	striped like a leopard	wild like a tiger

"**C**ats

Are

Terrific,"

Says Sam.

> **Can you think of any more adjectives to describe a cat?**

He has beautiful brown eyes.

soft, velvet fur	smooth, silky fur	a short, striped coat
long, black paws	a rough tongue	long, majestic whiskers
a cold, wet nose	a muscular body	a sparkling personality

> **Can you add any more?**

I am:

- stalking a little baby bird.
- creeping after a mouse in a bush.
- pouncing at a catnip mouse and rolling over and over with it.
- rolling my rattling ball along the hall.
- dribbling a ball in the garden, like a soccer player on T.V.
- purring loudly because my owner is tickling my tummy.
- yawning sleepily because I am worn out.
- climbing the curtains because I am feeling naughty.
- sleeping soundly in the chair.
- standing on the counter eating the hot chicken, while my owner is not looking.
- trying to look cute, so my owner gives me a piece of cheese.
- spilling my cat food on the floor.
- getting into a fight with my neighbor's cat because I don't like him.
- climbing the tree to the top, but I don't know how I'll get down.
- having an accident in the garage because I forgot I had a litter box.
- meowing at the top of my voice because I want to be noticed.
- scratching the chair because I WANT to sharpen my claws.
- hiding in the closet because I want some peace and quiet.
- stalking in the darkness because I love to hunt at night.

Who am I?

> **Write some more sentences that start I AM...** for your cat, rabbit, guinea pig, mouse, hamster, rat, spider, or any other animal you own.

Sam reads an *information leaflet* **persuading** pet lovers to get a kitten.

Lets get a **PET**!

If you want a pet that you will fall in love with from the moment you see him or her, choose a **silver tabby kitten**. They stare up at you with beautiful, piercing yellow eyes. They like you to stroke their striped fur as soft as silk.

They are loving family members who enjoy playing with young children and get along well with other animals in the home. If you let them out into the garden under supervision, they will race around like whirlwinds because they are lively and active. What's more, silver tabbies are never destructive and will not scratch holes in your sofa.

Jo says, "What I love about the silver tabby is their warm and affectionate personality. They have such appealing eyes and adore people."
"We have hours of fun," explains Matt, "playing with a fluffy toy on a stick. The energetic cat leaps into the air to get the toy."

If you want the cuddliest and cutest kitten ever, I'd recommend a silver tabby. You will be bringing into your house an intelligent cat that is lots of fun, very entertaining and who loves to be part of everything.

Read the information and write your own version. You can alter the names, the places, the things that happen. You can change the order, but make sure each sentence follows on from the one that went before. Use the plan on the next page.

MATCH

Expect:	information on looking after a pet
Find:	to make sure he is healthy
Visit:	to pay money
Check:	your pet in his home

If you want a pet that you will fall in love with from the moment you see him or her, choose a ……………………………………………………
………………………………………………………………………………………

They stare up at you with…………………………………………………………
………………………………………………………………………………………

They like you to………………………………………………………………………
………………………………………………………………………………………

They are loving family members who enjoy……………………………………
………………………………………………………………………………………

If you let them out into the garden, they will…………………………………
………………………………………………………………………………………
………………………………………………………………………………………

What's more,………………………………………………………………………
………………………………………………………………………………………

……………………………… says, "What I love about the…………………
………………………………………………………………………………………

"We have hours of fun," explains …………………………, "playing……..
………………………………………………………………………………………

If you want the cuddliest……………………………………………………………
………………………………………………………………………………………

I'd recommend a………………………………………………………………………

You will be bringing into your house……………………………………………
………………………………………………………………………………………

Mrs. Barker listens to Guinea Pig F.M. radio. She gets an **idea**. She will ask *the children in her class to talk about* their **funny animal stories**.

- My neighbor's parrot screeches so loudly that I cannot concentrate on my homework.

- My cat sits on my math book, so I can't study for my test.

That is a good excuse, Lee.

- We have to check our dryer, our washing machine and our dishwasher because Bubbles our kitten likes to hide in them.

- My gran's kitten hangs on the curtain clumsily and he tears a hole in it.

- Our cat waits for us to come home. When he hears the car coming up to the driveway, he runs out and rolls over and over.

- My cat climbs onto my mom's shoulder and watches her do the dishes.

- Some hedgehogs used to get into our garbage bag and lick out empty containers of rice pudding.

- My dog brought in an old sandwich that he had found in the trash and sat eating it in front of the T.V.

- Our cat is not allowed on the bed, so he sneaks upstairs when he thinks no one is looking and sprawls right across the blanket, with a silly look on his face. Then my mom goes crazy.

- My cat can retrieve a mouse like a dog. If I throw it, he will go and get it in his teeth and bring it back to me – but only if he gets a treat.

- My auntie's dog growls at the mailman fiercely, and when he puts the letters through the door, he chews them up.

- We put some chicken bones down for a family of foxes and then we watched them gobble them up.

- My cat is a gymnast. She could win a gold medal. She waits in the corner to pounce on her multicolored mouse on a stick. We pull it speedily along the carpet and then lift it high in the air. Then Lucy runs and turns a somersault to catch it. Even more than this, she likes the feather duster. When Mom dusts, she runs, jumps and pounces at it, so the colored feathers fly everywhere. I think she is pretending she is a bird.

Make a Pet File with *facts about a pet*. If you do not have a pet of your own, write about the pet of a friend, a neighbor, a family member or just imagine that you have a pet.

Owner: ……………………………………………………………………………………

Pet's name:…………………………………………………………………………………

He/She is cute because:………(focus on appearance: ears, face, whiskers, coat)

………………………………………………………………………………………………

His/Her most mischievous moment was:………………(focus on character)

The smartest thing he or she did was:……………………………………………

He/She hates to:……………………….loves to:…………………………………

He/She is cute, loving, kind, proud or mean:………………..…………..

He/She sleeps in:…………………………………. (focus on what he or she does)

He/She eats:………………………………………………………………………………

He/She hunts:………………………………………………………………………………

Funny things he/she does are:……………..……………………………………

Mrs. Barker puts her **best stories** on the wall.

Frank writes a story about how he took care of his friend's pet.

Read the story and write your own version. You can alter:

- the names
- the places
- the things that happen

I have never liked snakes and I don't know what got into me when I offered to take care of Jake's anaconda for the weekend. Little did I know what I was getting myself into. The green snake, which measures 16 feet in length, comes from the Amazon rainforest, so I was not too happy to have him in our small semi-detached house. On the day when he was due to arrive, I arose early to clean up the kitchen to make room for his cage. Before I knew it, Jake was banging on the door and thrusting Fred's heavy cage at me.

Anxiously, I heaved the cage into the kitchen. I peered through the bars and met Fred's eye. He had a menacing look in his bright eyes. I knew I didn't need to feed him, since snakes only eat once a week, but Fred (who definitely had other ideas) was hungry. I settled him down in his cage in the corner of the kitchen and I went out of the room to get a book, 'How to Keep a Snake.' When I returned a few moments later, Fred had escaped. He was up on the counter. He was about to pounce on my pet hamster and swallow him down in one gulp. I managed to grab him just in time; I put him back in his cage. He calmed down and went to sleep, so I went upstairs to play on my PlayStation. An hour later, I came down but he was nowhere to be seen. His cage was empty. Fred was high up on the ceiling wrapped around an electric light. He was so high that I could not reach him.
"Oh no!" I cried to myself, "I will never get him down from there."

There was only one way to get Fred down and that was to call the fire department. Fifteen minutes later, the fire engine arrived outside my house with its bright flashing lights. The fireman knocked on my door.
"What's the problem?" he asked sternly.
"My snake is wrapped around the light up there," I pointed.
"That's a tricky one...Is he friendly?" he continued rather apprehensively.
"I don't know," I replied. "I'm taking care of him for a friend." The fireman climbed to the top of his ladder and put one hand out. Fred met his eye and gave him a menacing look. The fireman reached out two hands to grab him. At that instant, Fred slithered slyly away from the light, did a belly flop down onto the cabinet, then down onto the counter, then onto the floor and back into his cage. We both looked on in amazement, as he settled down to sleep. I stammered,
"Thank you for your help," but the fireman left the house quickly, muttering that I should not have wasted a fireman's time.
The next day, when I took Fred back to Jake, I never mentioned the events of the weekend, but I vowed never to take care of a snake again.

Now it is your turn to write a story called **The day I took care of my friend's pet**.

Get used to making a plan.

Character: I, snake, friend   *(write in first person)*

Setting: home

Plot: taking care of a pet, but things go wrong

Paragraphs:

Beginning

- agreed to take care of a friend's pet
- it was a 16 foot snake
- cleaned up kitchen to make room for his cage
- friend brought Fred around

Middle

- peered into Fred's cage
- had a menacing look
- seemed to be hungry
- escaped from his cage
- threatened to pounce on pet hamster
- escaped from cage a second time
- curled himself around the light

Ending

- called fire department in a panic
- fireman knocked on door
- brought a ladder to rescue Fred - rather apprehensively
- snake slithered back down into cage by himself
- told not to waste fireman's time
- decided to never take care of a snake again

You can use the unfinished sentences on the next page to help you write your story.

- Little did I know what I was getting myself into, when I offered to...

- The snake was a...

- It was the day he was due to arrive, so ...

- Soon my friend was banging at...

- I heaved the heavy cage into the...

- The snake looked at me with...

- He seemed hungry, but...

- I left the room to get...

- When I came back he had...

   and was about to...

- I put him back in... and...

- An hour later, I came downstairs and found him...

- "Oh no!" I said. I will have to call...

- Fifteen minutes later, the ...

- The fireman looked up at.................... He muttered, "...................."

- Then he climbed his ladder to...

  but the naughty snake...

- By this time the fireman was...

- Later I took Fred back ...

- I decided...

Why I should have stayed in bed.

On Saturday, I woke to the sound of screams coming from downstairs.
"Ah! There is a snake in the laundry hamper and it just bit me!" screamed Mom in a panic. I jumped out of bed and ran downstairs to see what all the fuss was about.
"Cecil," I yelled, "I thought I had lost you." Cecil was my pet snake. He had escaped from his cage two days ago and I thought I would never see him again. I put him back in his cage and left Mom to finish the laundry.

Now, I sat down for breakfast, ready to tuck into delicious pancakes, but I did not know what hid in the juicy batter.
"These pancakes are not good today," said my sister. I looked down at my plate in horror and saw… MAGGOTS! YUCK!
"Mom, there are maggots in the pancakes!" I gasped. "I'm not eating them."
"Don't be silly," replied Mom. "How could there possibly be maggots in the pancakes?" Everybody stared down at their plates. There was a horrible silence and then the house was full of screams.

Little did I know what the rest of the day would bring. After the snake and maggot incident, everything seemed to be going smoothly, but then came a cry from the upstairs bathroom.
"There is a huge spider on the toilet seat," shouted Dad. "It's huge, it's furry and as big as a tarantula." I raced up to my bedroom where I kept Jenny. She's not everyone's idea of a good pet. Guess what… the tank was open:
"Oh no, I am really in for it this time." I knew I should have stayed in bed.

By Oliver

Now it's your turn to write a story: 'Why I Should Have Stayed In Bed.'

Get used to making a plan.

Characters: (I), Mom, Dad, family with children

Setting: a home

Plot: creepy crawly creatures cause problems

Paragraphs:

Beginning

- narrator woke up
- Mom was screaming
- snake was in laundry hamper
- it's Cecil - a lost pet snake
- missing for two days

Middle

- eating breakfast
- enjoying delicious pancakes
- saw maggots in them
- everyone was disgusted

Ending

- Dad found enormous spider on toilet seat
- my tank of exotic pets was open
- should have stayed in bed

You can use the unfinished sentences on the next page to help you write a story.

How to write a story:

- The story is written in first person (I).
- It is told from the writer's point of view.
- The first paragraph introduces the characters, setting and plot.
- Each paragraph deals with a separate problem, occurring at a different time of the day.

- The middle builds up a series of exciting events.
- Actions move the story along.
- End the second paragraph with a problem to create tension.

- Wind the story up with a third problem.
- Bring it to a conclusion that the reader will understand.

- On Saturday I woke to the sound of…

- "Eeek! There's a… in the…" screamed Mom.

- I ran downstairs to see…

- It was Cecil, my pet snake, causing the trouble… because he was...

- "You're not lost," I said, as I...

....

- Next, I sat down for breakfast…

- Mom brought in a steaming plate of… but when I looked down I saw…

- I complained that…

- Mom replied…

- Everyone stared at their plate...

- There was… and then...

....

- After the (snake and the maggot) incidents everything seemed…

- Then a voice came from…

- It said, "There is a… on…

- Oh no! I said to myself. It could be...

- I ran up to check my tank of exotic pets, but...

- I should have...

Theo

"Where is Theo?" shouted Fran. "Theo, Theo, Theo," she called frantically. He seemed to be missing, so she started to search the house. She went into the garden to look for him, but he was not there. He was not sitting by the pond, or hiding in his favorite spot in the shed and there was no sign of him in the street. Fran was filled with panic.

Next morning, Theo had still not turned up. Fran drove around the streets and knocked on neighbors' doors to ask if they had seen him. She called, "Theo, Theo, Theo," but there was no sign of him anywhere. She felt gloomy. Was he lost? Had he been stolen? Had he wandered into someone's shed and gotten trapped? Then she heard something. It was a faint meow. It was coming from a hole in the hedge. Suddenly, she saw Theo's head sticking out. He had been trying to squeeze through a hole, but he was stuck.

After this, Fran tried to pull Theo out, but he would not budge. Theo was greedy and loved to eat. He was also lazy and spent a lot of time sleeping, so he was very fat. What's more, he didn't like being trapped, so he hissed and hissed. Then a neighbor arrived home and Fran explained the problem. Together they tugged and tugged and tugged… and eventually the fat cat popped out of the hole. Fran was so relieved. Theo was cuddled, stroked and kissed. Do you think he had learned a lesson from his adventure? No! He only wanted a bowl of his favorite cat food.

Now it's your turn to write a story called 'Lost.'

Get used to making a rough plan.

Characters: A cat owner - Fran

Setting: A garden and street

Plot: A cat is lost and then found.

Paragraphs:

Beginning

- cat Theo was missing
- Fran searched garden, house, shed
- lost cat didn't turn up
- panic

Middle

- next morning cat was still missing
- Fran knocked on neighbors' doors
- searched the neighborhood
- very worried
- heard meow
- saw her cat's head sticking out of a hole in the hedge
- stuck

Ending

- Fran tried to pull cat out
- cat was too fat to go through hole - cat hissed
- neighbor helped to tug cat out
- cat was rescued, but only wanted food - had not learned his lesson

---

- The story is written in third person - she, he, they.
- The introduction introduces characters, setting and plot.

- The middle paragraph has a series of actions.
- There is a problem to solve and suspense is built up.

- The story is wound up with a happy ending.

You can use the unfinished sentences to help you write a story.

- "Where is Theo?" shouted…

- He was missing, so Fran...

    but he was not in the... or in the...

- In fact, he wasn't anywhere...

- so Fran was...

....

- Next morning, Theo still hadn't...

- Fran drove around the streets to see if...

- She was worried that...

- After a little while, she heard a meow... coming from...

- He was...

....

- Fran tried to pull...

    but he was too...

- He hissed because...

- Finally, a neighbor helped to...

Sam describes the time they took care of Auntie's
MONSTER

Monster had a sad expression when Auntie Maddy brought him to stay, while she went on vacation. It changed to a grin the moment her car sped off to the airport. Before we had even shut the front door, Monster was growling ferociously at our cat.

"Give him some of the doggie biscuits," suggested Dad. At the word biscuit, Monster's ears pricked up and his tail wagged excitedly. He bounded up to me and he sat on his hind legs in a begging position. He placed his paws on my chest and, with his tongue hanging out, he proceeded to wolf down the whole packet of biscuits, until there were none left. Then, he looked around for something else to do...

"How about a nice walk?" said Mom. "He needs exercise to use up some of his energy," she added, as she dangled his collar and leash in front of him. Monster went wild. He approved of this walk. We set out for the local park, stopping frequently so Monster could sniff each lamp post. Once we were through the iron gate at the park, we slipped off his collar and leash, so he could run free. He did run; he bolted across the grass like a sprinter, to greet other dogs.

"Can you keep your dog under control?" protested an angry dog walker. But it was too late, Monster had taken on more than he could chew.* He had gotten into a big fight with a huge dog. This dog was coming closer. He was snarling viciously at Monster. He was about to tear him to pieces with his sharp teeth.
"No Monster. Naughty boy. Come here!" we commanded.

More than he could chew - is an idiom and means he had taken on more than he could cope with.

Eventually, Mom and I managed to drag Monster away from the fight with the angry dog. "Fetch the ball, Monster," we ordered. "Go get it, boy... Bring it back," but he seemed to have no interest in ball games. Instead, he preferred a chase. He raced away, and then waited for us to catch up. He raced away again, but... then he got bored of this teasing game, too... That's when he saw a hole in the fence. It was just big enough for him to squeeze into. He disappeared through it as quick as a shot, leaving Mom and I looking stupid. We trudged back home with an empty leash and no dog. Had we lost Auntie Maddy's precious dog? How would we explain? Imagine our surprise when we arrived home to see Monster already waiting on the doorstep, grinning at us, as if to say - I won.

Now it's your turn to write a story called, 'Taking Care of a Naughty Pet.'

Get used to making a plan.

Character: Auntie Maddy, Mom, Dad, me, bad dog

Settings: Moves from home, to street, to park.

Plot: A family was watching a dog while the owner was on vacation, but the dog was naughty and caused problems at home and in the park.

Paragraphs:

Beginning

- Monster was sad because his owners had left him
- had naughty expression
- chased cat
- sat and begged for food
- wolfed food down

Middle

- walked to park
- sniffed lamp post
- raced off yapping
- annoyed another dog and its owner
- got into a fight with a big dog
  who growled and showed his teeth

Ending

- the dog sitters dragged him away from the fight
- the dog wouldn't retrieve the ball
- the dog wanted to play chase
- went through hole in fence
- the dog sitters thought they'd lost him and went home alone
- Monster sat on doorstep when they arrived home

- *The story is written in first person.*
- *The first paragraph introduces characters, setting and clues about the kind of dog they are looking after, so the reader realizes the dog is very difficult.*

- *A series of events builds up as the dog behaves badly.*
- *Tension mounts as the dog gets into a fight.*

- *The story is wound up with a happy ending.*

- Monster had a sad expression when…

    but…

- Before we shut the front door he was…
- Dad said, "Give him some…
- He bounded up to me and…
- Then, he gobbled down…

- "How about a walk," asked Mom to…
- Monster went wild because he…
- We set out for the park, but…
- When we got through the gate, we…
- He raced across the grass towards…
- A dog owner protested, "Can you keep…

    but it was too late; Monster had gotten into a fight with…

- The huge dog was…

- We dragged Monster back to…

    but he refused to…

- He preferred to play a game of…

    but he got bored quickly and found a…

- We were worried because we thought…

    but…

- Imagine our surprise when…

Our cat Henriki is as playful as a kitten. His favorite toy is his catnip mouse. When he sniffs it, he goes crazy. First, he takes it between his paws, licks it all over until it's soggy and then he rolls over and over. Next, he bites it hard and kicks it with his back legs.

Henriki also loves to play with a multicolored mouse on a stick. We take turns pulling it slowly along the carpet, until he pounces. Sometimes, we swing it through the air, so he leaps high to catch it. He punches it with his paw and turns a somersault in the air. Then he looks back to see if anyone is looking because he's a real show off.

More than this, his favorite game is chasing the feather duster around. When we dust the stairs, he leaps through the gaps in the banister, grabs it with his teeth and sends the blue feathers flying all over the carpet - as if he had caught a real bluebird. Then he sits guarding the feathers. This makes him really tired, so he curls up and goes to sleep with feathers still poking out from under his fur.

Write some paragraphs saying what your pet does.

'Lost'

I remember that cold November night when a stray kitten arrived on our doorstep. Where he had come from, nobody knew. He was cold, he was hungry and he was a stranger wandering through the night. The stray cat, without a home, stopped to watch us unload our groceries and then he followed us into the kitchen. When I opened the fridge door, he sniffed the air. The scent of fresh chicken made him crazy. Was he starving? Had he not eaten for days? I opened the cabinet door under the sink, where I stored our cat's food, and he rubbed his feather-light body around my legs. I offered him just a few dried biscuits. He gobbled them down. Now he turned and looked up at me thankfully, with big, brown eyes that pleaded for just a few more. I left the front door open so that he could go back into the darkness, but he seemed reluctant to leave.

Instead, he made himself comfortable in our house. He went upstairs and he curled himself up on the landing carpet, where he slept soundly all night long. When he awoke, he was in fine spirits. He went down to the living room and there he fought the chair legs with his claws, leaped after our cat's mouse and rolled over and over. Next, he raced across our polished kitchen floor like a crazy cat and skidded to a halt, to avoid banging his head on the wall. He gobbled down every piece of cat food, including our cat's breakfast. Now our cat appeared. She was hungry too. She was very concerned that her breakfast had been eaten. Who was this creature who had eaten it? She snarled, she hissed, she chased him around the kitchen. I opened the front door again, but he refused to leave. HE HAD COME TO STAY.

Despite our cat's effort to get rid of the new kitten, which was threatening her territory, the kitten had made himself at home. Everyone loved him and he was enjoying all the strokes, the cuddles and the tummy tickles. A few days later, we decided to take him for a health check.

"He's beautiful," the veterinary nurse gasped. "I wish we could keep him here."

"He's a fine fellow," commented the vet. "He's a pedigree. Let's see if he's micro chipped; that will tell us where he has come from... No, there's not one. Imagine letting a lovely cat like this wander off, though I must say, he's in fine health."

"What should we do?" we asked.

"You have a choice," replied the vet. "Take him to the ASPCA or keep him at home. You could ask around the streets or put up some posters to see if anyone has lost a cat. I'll put him on the database for lost cats, but if no one comes forward he's yours...." This is what we did, but no one claimed him. Now he's grown up into a handsome cat, with stripes and long paws. He's made friends with our cat. Well, most of the time!

How do you think this cat got lost?
Tell his story.

Get used to making a plan.

Character: (I) first person, stray kitten, family

Setting: moves from unloading groceries out of the car - to house - to vet

Plot: a stray cat finds a home

Paragraphs:

Beginning

- a cat turned up on doorstep
- it was dark - he was a stray
- desperately hungry
- begged for food

Middle

- wouldn't leave
- made himself comfortable at home
- played with toys - showed off
- ate more food
- ate our cat's dinner
- got into fight with our cat

Ending

Vet said:
- he was a very special cat
- he was in good health
- should take him to ASPCA or keep him
- put up signs, ask around
- put him on lost cat database
- keep him if not claimed
- now we have two cats

- It was a cold November night and…

- A kitten arrived on…

- First, he followed us into the kitchen because...

    so I gave him…

- Then, he looked at me with big eyes, pleading for…

- That night he slept on…

    When he awoke next morning, he went into the living room where he …

- Next, he went to the kitchen to...

- Suddenly, our cat appeared because…

- She saw the other cat and she…

- Soon she was... but...

- Two days layer, everyone had fallen in love with…   so we...

- The vet said he was…

- He advised us to...

- His owner never claimed him, so we...

An Interview with MONSTER the dog

What did you think when you found your owner had a new cat?

> I thought we could play. My cat runs so I think she wants me to chase her. It's a good game.

Do you think you scare your cat?

> No! We play exciting games. My cat likes to balance on a high perch like a shelf. Then I yap at her. She's so high up that I can't catch her. We're going to be friends.

Imagine animals can talk like humans.
Write an interview between two animals.

An Interview with 'Millie' the cat

What did you think when your owner got a dog?

"I WAS SCARED."

Why?

"HE WANTS TO PLAY ALL THE TIME. HE DOESN'T UNDERSTAND THE WORD NO. HE'S TOO MUCH - TOO BOISTEROUS."

Do you like him now?

"HE CHASES ME SO I HAVE TO SIT HIGH ON A SHELF AND I CAN'T GET DOWN. HE'S ALWAYS RUNNING AROUND WILDLY: TONGUE OUT, WAGGING HIS TAIL AND BARKING AT THE TOP OF HIS VOICE. I LIKE TO BE CALM, TO BE STROKED, TO BE CUDDLED, TO THINK QUIETLY. I THOUGHT OF LEAVING HOME."

Do you think you could ever be friends?

"MAYBE ONE DAY, BUT ONLY IF HE LEAVES MY FOOD ALONE... AND MY BED... AND MY TOYS... AND GIVES ME SOME SPACE."

Rushford's local newspaper has a pet problem page. Raj your local vet is on hand to answer your questions.

RUSHFORD PROBLEM PAGE

Dear Raj,

Our cat spends all his time stretched out on the bed. He hardly ever ventures out, only to use the litter box. He never wants to play, never wants to be stroked, but only wants to sleep all the time.

I am worried because when he was a kitten, he used to race around with a jingly ball, hitting it with his paws. He used to run and pounce on his toys, but now he seems to have no energy at all.

Please can you advise me how we can make him playful again? How can we make him want to climb to the top of the tree and pounce on a bird?

Cat Lover from Rushford

Dear Cat Lover from Rushford,

Your cat sounds a bit depressed. To help cheer him up, I suggest you play pouncing games. Use cat toys, such as: feathers on string, a fishing rod toy, which you drag enticingly in front of his line of vision. A few minutes a day would help cheer him up and he would have a fun time with his owners.

Raj

PROBLEM PAGE

Dear Raj,

We are planning to go away for two weeks to France and have booked our eight month old puppy, Isaac, into the local kennel. I am very worried about leaving him because he has never been in this kind of environment before. I am afraid he will get upset and not settle down.

You see, Isaac, who has always been very nervous of other people, prefers to stay inside the house with our family. In fact, he likes to sleep in my son's bedroom and curl up beside his bed in his basket. He never leaves my nine year old son, even when he is on the computer.

Is there anything I can do to make it easy for him? Is there anything I can take to remind him of us? I am so worried that my family is considering canceling our vacation. I will not enjoy the vacation knowing that he is so unhappy. Can you advise me what I should do?

Concerned Dog Lover Mom

Write a reply from Raj.

....
....
....
....
....
....
....
....
....
....
....
....

Now, write a letter to Raj to get advice about your pet or about an animal - maybe a wild animal, such as a bird or squirrel in your garden.

○ **Kim reads an article in the cat magazine. It gives some instructions:**

- **Groom** your pet for a short time each day.

- **Use** a comb to remove loose hair.

- **Tease out** knots in the fur with your fingers.

- **Find** a warm place, where your pet will be comfortable.

- **Buy** a natural shampoo to soap up your cat in the bath.

It is your turn to write some instructions on how to care for a pet. Use bossy words, called imperatives, like:

Buy...   Groom...   Use...

Now use your imagination. **Invent some delicious treats** for animals. Maybe some tasty new food for dogs or yummy biscuits for cats. Be creative. **Make an ad for your new food.**

Remember to say:
- **what is in your treat,**
- **why animals will love it so much,**
- **why it is better than other products.**

Draw a picture of your treat.

Here is an example:

YUMMY!

A TASTY NEW BISCUIT FOR DOGS:

- Filled with vitamins, to make your dog's coat shine.

- It has a delicious meaty taste.

- It is shaped like bones.

- Recommended by vets.

Your dog will love it.

Sam sees a competition advertised in the newspaper. It reads:

> Calling all budding inventors. Invent a product for your pet. It can be as 'weird' and 'wacky' as you like. The winning entry will be made and sold in top pet stores around the country.

Sam is excited. He has lots of ideas.

1. **A satellite navigation homing device** - This device fixes on your pet's collar. It tells you exactly where your pet is at all times and you will never lose your pet again. If your cat sneaks off to avoid the vet's appointment, it's not a problem because the revolutionary satellite navigation homing device will pinpoint your cat's hiding place.

2. **A time release cat feeder** – This device releases food at a time set by you. Greedy cats and dogs can never gobble all their food up at once because food is released slowly - bit by bit.

3. A beautiful set of **light up cushions and blankets** for your pet to cuddle up in.

4. A **DVD that teaches your parrot to talk**. It plays funny phrases over and over again, so your parrot can copy them. Soon your bird will be chattering non-stop.

5. A **cat activity center** – which has fun toys for your cat to play with.

6. A remote control bird for cats – which will give your pet hours of fun dashing around the house trying to catch it.

7. An amazing pet bed. Can you describe it?
   ....
   ....
   ....

Now it is your turn. You can develop one of Sam's ideas or invent a product yourself. Happy inventing!

1. Draw a detailed picture of your invention.

2. Label the main features.

3. Write how the product works.

4. What are the main features?

5. Why have you invented it?

6. Is it unique?

7. Why is it better than other products?

A <u>sad</u> story with a **happy** ending.

New Home

One day Tiggy's owner took him to the parking lot by the dark woods to a place he didn't recognize. He tied him to a post. As he drove away he mumbled, "I'm sorry, I have no money to care for you." The sun went down. Tiggy waited and waited in the dark for his owner, but he didn't come back.

Tiggy whimpered sadly because he didn't know what to do. He barked loudly calling for help. His stomach was empty. He felt weak with hunger. Soon he became so exhausted that he flopped down on the ground. There, he dreamed of his warm blanket, his squeaky toys and his food bowl filled to the top with juicy morsels of meat. Nobody came for him. He lay shivering in the cold for hours. Suddenly, Tiggy raised an ear; he could hear footsteps approaching. They were getting nearer and nearer. He felt a warm hand stroke him gently and he heard some kind words.

Someone untied him, put a collar on him and put him in the back of a white van, which said 'Animal Rescue.' They took him back to the center. The people were so kind to him there that he soon felt better. They gave him a new warm bed, a new toy and a bowl of delicious food. The next day a lady came to see Tiggy in his kennel. She threw his ball playfully and he fetched it back, which made her laugh loudly. Tiggy felt happy because he knew he had met his new owner and soon she would take him to his new home.

If you want to help sad dogs like Tiggy, support the work of Rushford Animal Trust. If you give just $5 a month, it will provide food, bedding and medicine to help sad dogs that have been abandoned. You will make them happy again.

Write a persuasive ad to encourage people to help an animal. Tell a story and then make an appeal for money or help. For another idea you could tell people why they must not buy animals as a Christmas present.

Cut out or copy the story prompts below. Mix them up and arrange them in order, so your story has a beginning, a middle and an end. Then re-write the story, adding your own ideas to it.

It was Saturday night

---

and we were driving to a restaurant.

My cousin Paula slammed on the brakes

---

because there were four horses galloping in the road.

They had escaped. What should we do?

Paula called the police on her cell phone.

She told the drivers, who were behind her, that there was danger ahead.

One of them got out of her car and tried to coax the horses onto the shoulder, but they were terrified.

In a few minutes the police arrived with sirens flashing and closed the road.

By this time, there was a huge traffic jam and people were coming out of their houses to watch.

The police contacted a local farmer who owned a trailer for horses. He came immediately.

Everyone watched the farmer chase the horses down the road, calm them down and get them into the trailer.

Later, the scared horses were relieved to be back safely in their own field.

The publisher permits you to copy the pages containing cut out story prompts.
No other pages of this book may be copied.

Cut out or copy the story prompts below. Mix them up and arrange them in order, so your story has a beginning, a middle and an end. Then re-write the story, adding your own ideas to it.

The moon was shining brightly.

Hedgehog woke up.

He padded through the fallen leaves.

"I'll explore the garden," he said to himself

---

and he shuffled slowly across the lawn and up the path.

As he passed the house, he watched giant moths buzzing,

---

bats skimming above him

---

and an owl flying silently by.

He swallowed down a slimy slug.
"That was delicious," he muttered to himself.

Suddenly, there was a scary sound nearby.

The front door opened and he heard human voices very close.

They said,
"Look! Isn't he sweet."

Sensing some danger, he curled up into a tight ball.

"Don't touch me. I'm covered with prickly spines," he warned them.

There he remained until dawn broke

and the first rays of sun warmed his back.

Then slowly, very slowly, he uncurled.

What did he see? There was a big saucer of milk in a huge bowl.

He lapped it up before returning home to bed.

"Humans are not so bad after all," he thought.

Cut out or copy the story prompts below. Mix them up and arrange them in order, so your story has a beginning, a middle and an end. Then re-write the story, adding your own ideas to it.

No one ever bothered to lock Charlie's cage. He was free to come and go as he pleased, but not everyone agreed.

Rat was busy in his cage.

He nibbled his cereal greedily,

---

scrambled wildly in his straw,

---

played excitedly on his wheel

---

and then looked around for something else to do.

For a moment he stopped to listen.

There was a strange noise nearby.

It was a whistling sound.

There was a man mending some leaking pipes over by the sink and he was making a tune with his lips.

Rat wanted to say hello,

so he scampered through the unlocked door of his cage and poked his nose into the man's foot.

"Eeek!" yelled the plumber.

"Is there a problem?" yelled Mom.

"Is there a burst pipe?" shouted Dad.

"...I thought I saw a horrible rat," stammered the plumber,

as he dropped his screwdriver on the floor.

"I have a phobia of rodents – especially rats."

"That's only Charlie," they reassured him.
"He just wants to help."

But the terrified man had run out of the door.

Sam and Frank learn about **polar bears** for their school project. Use the polar bear facts below to write an information leaflet about the polar bear. You can find some more facts on the internet or in a reference book. Put the facts below in the right order.

ABOUT ME

BY A MOTHER POLAR BEAR

- I **live in the Arctic** on the ice caps.

- It is **freezing cold** here with **thick ice**.

- I **hunt for seals** in the frozen sea.

- My **cubs are born under the ice**, where I **build a den in a snow bank.**

- My **cubs drink my milk, while I live on my baby fa**t. When my **cubs are old enough to leave the den, I hunt for food.**

Use headings to help you

- Where I live
- What I am like
- My babies
- Why I am endangered

- My **thick, oily fur keeps me warm** when I swim in the frozen sea.

- As a polar bear, I can be **dangerous to people.**

- **P**e**ople can also be dangerous** to polar bears.

- We are **protected from hunters by laws**.

- I am <u>**IN DANGER**</u> as a species.

- The **ice caps are melting because of global warming**. It is dangerous because it **damages our habitat**.

- Humans are **mining and drilling** and they have **caused pollution**, which is very harmful.

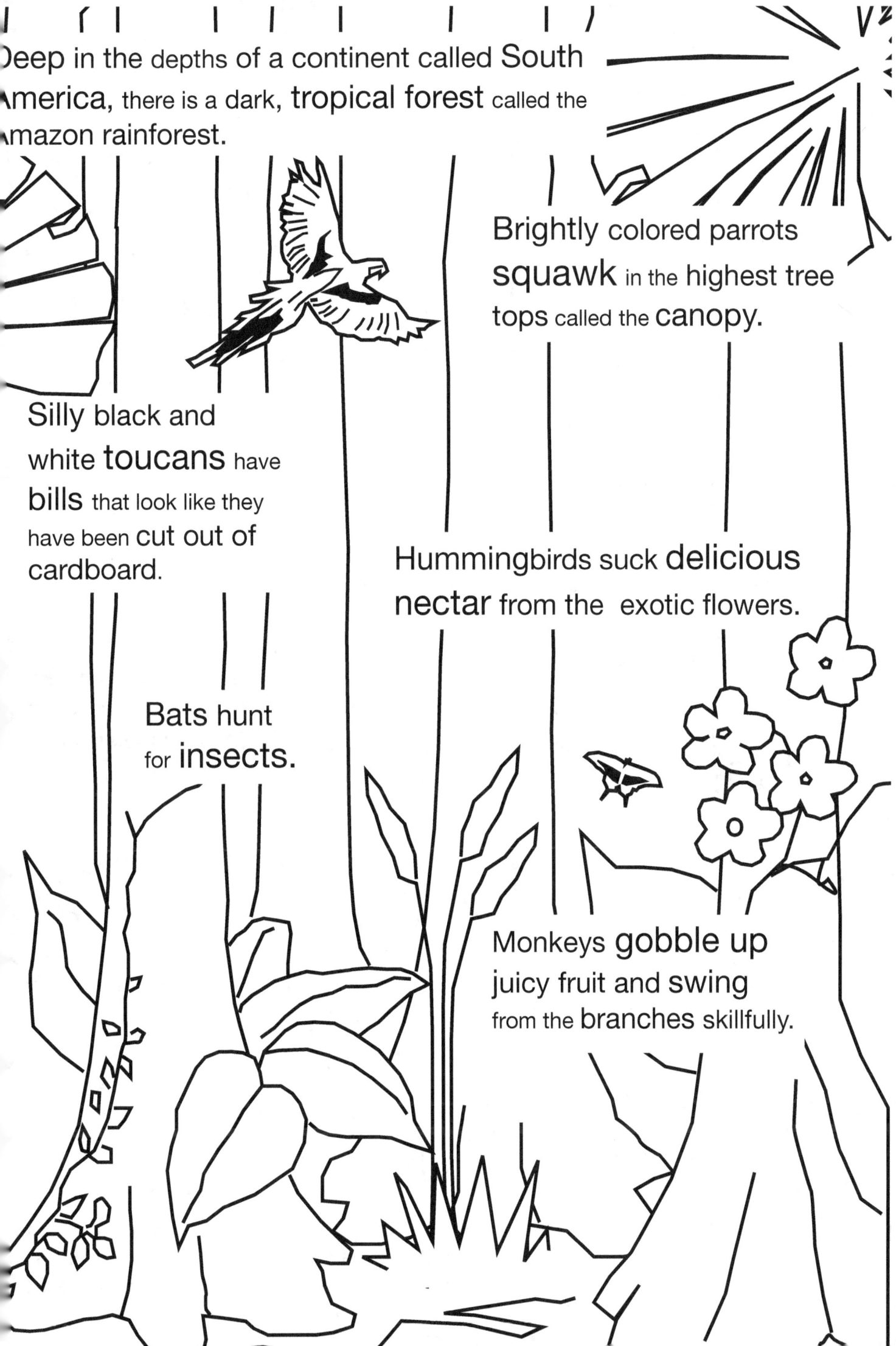

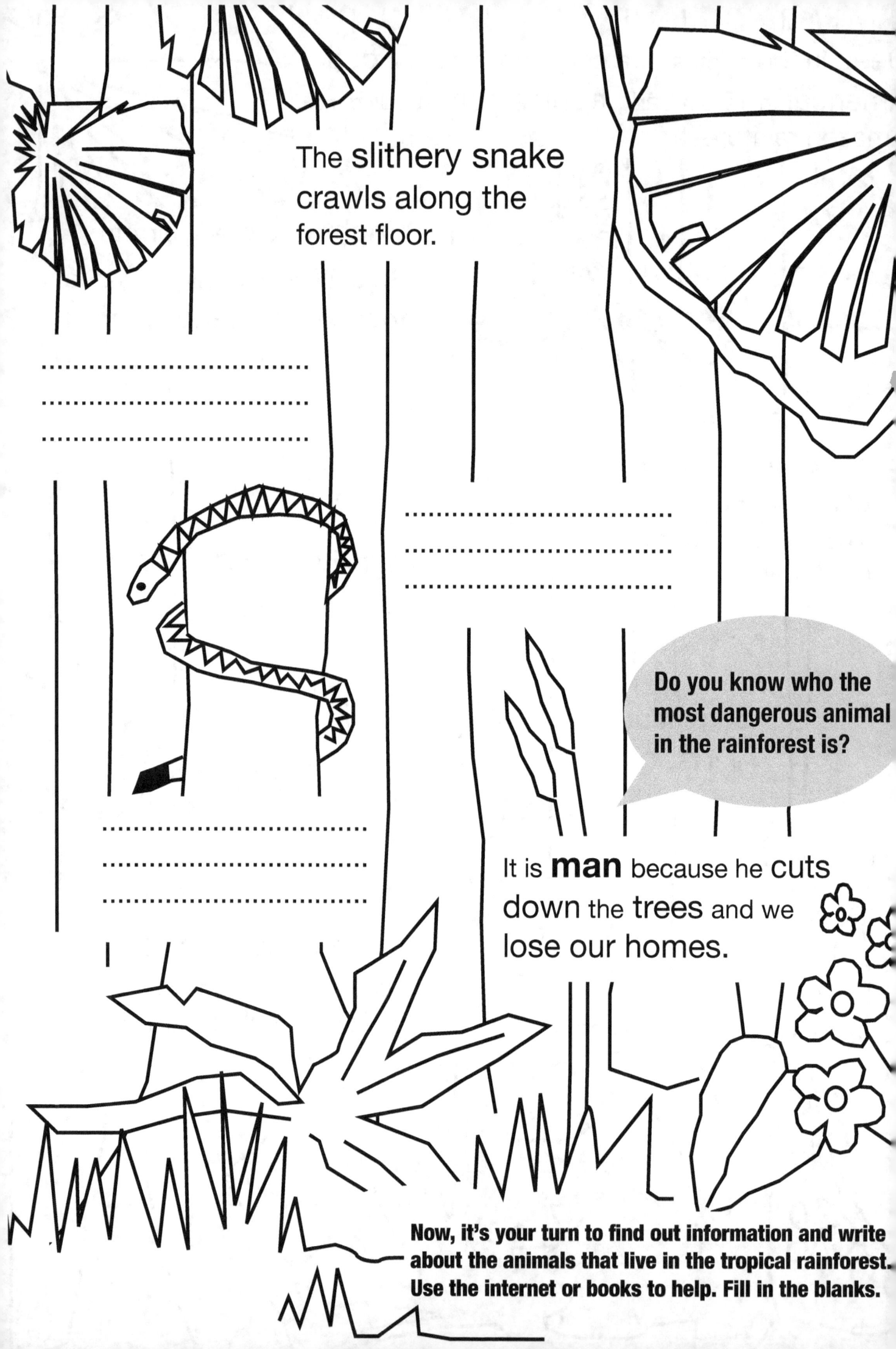

> # Write an information leaflet about the Amazon rainforest.
>
> - Use subheadings to help your reader find information quickly.
> - Write in sentences. Use the notes to help you.

Where is the Amazon rainforest?

The Amazon rainforest is in South America.

What is the climate like there?

- hot
- wet
- near the equator
- every day the same
- no seasons like autumn, summer, spring or winter

What it is like in the Amazon rainforest?

vivid colors   evergreen trees   bright flowers   rich habitat

dense jungle   loud squawking birds

warm   wet   humid temperatures   dark (on forest floor)

gnarled trees   colossal leaves

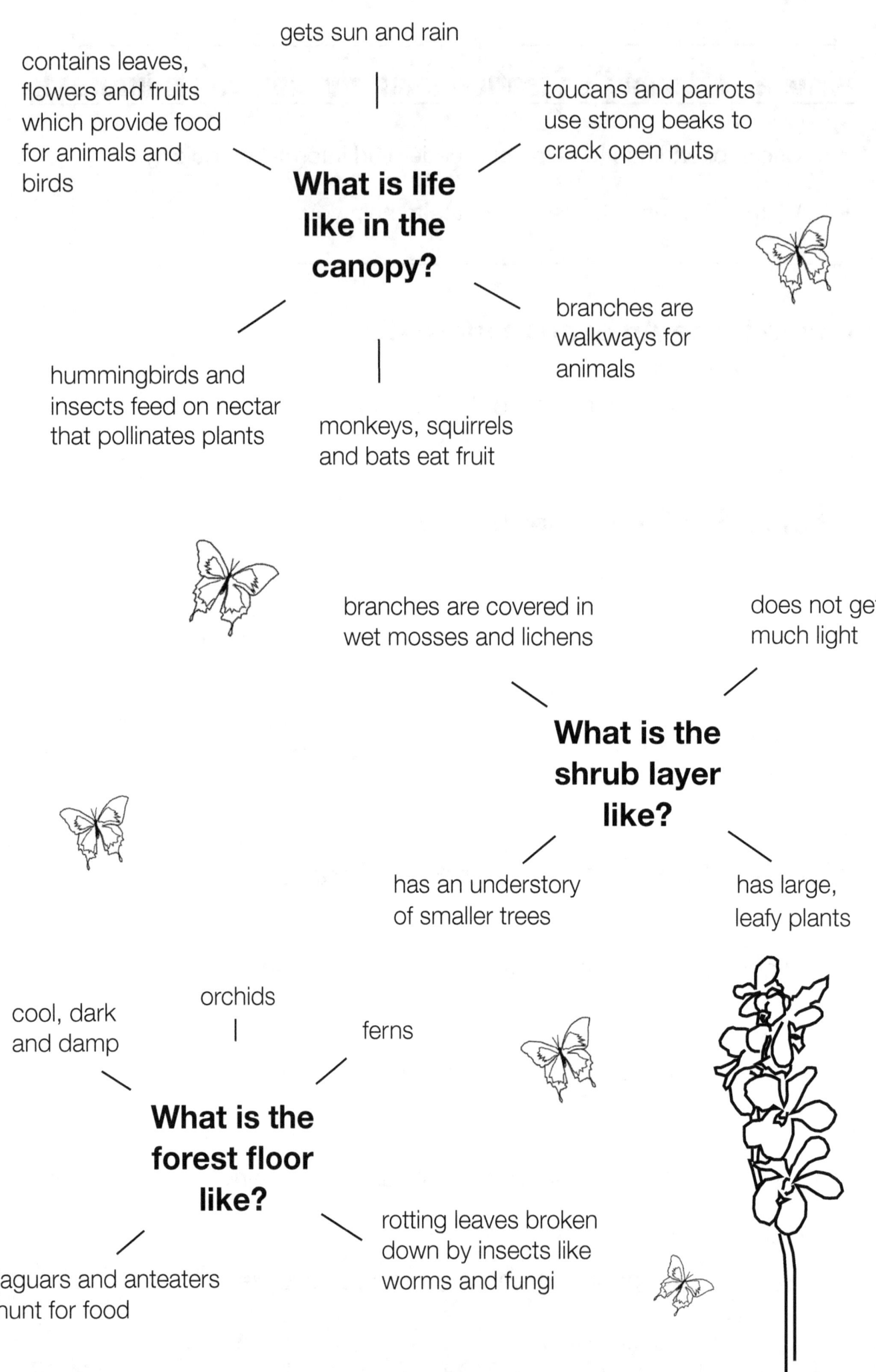

Animals that live in the Amazon rainforest

Match the animal to its activity. Fill in the chart below.

Which animal am I?

Anteaters	Ambushes tasty prey in the branches.
Sloths	Screech loudly
Jaguars	Long sticky tongue probes ant nest.
Tapirs	Snacks on favorite passion fruit.
Snakes like Boa Constrictors	Flies by twisting and turning.
Countless insects	....
Hummingbirds	....
Toucans	....
Parrots	....
Eagles	....
Monkeys	....

(Anteaters → Long sticky tongue probes ant nest.)

Write a **leaflet** to persuade people to come to a wildlife park called <u>Rainforest World.</u>

Use three paragraphs

Paragraph 1

- Who will enjoy going there?
    - parents
    - children
    - teachers
- What is the purpose of going there?
    - To learn about the South American rainforest
    - Where it is
    - What the climate is like
    - Explore by going into a forest

Paragraph 2

- What will you see?
    - animals and their babies
- What will you discover?
    - facts like the anteater has a long probing tongue which he flicks 300 times a minute
- What will you experience?
    - a hot tropical house where animals live and where you can walk around
- How will you relax?
    - in a South American cafe with great party ideas
- What can you buy?
    - gifts such as a parrot keychain

Paragraph 3

- How much does it cost?
- Where is it?
- When is it open?
- Which times?

Rainforest World

Make a map of the center.

Use your imagination to think up some attractions. Here is an example.

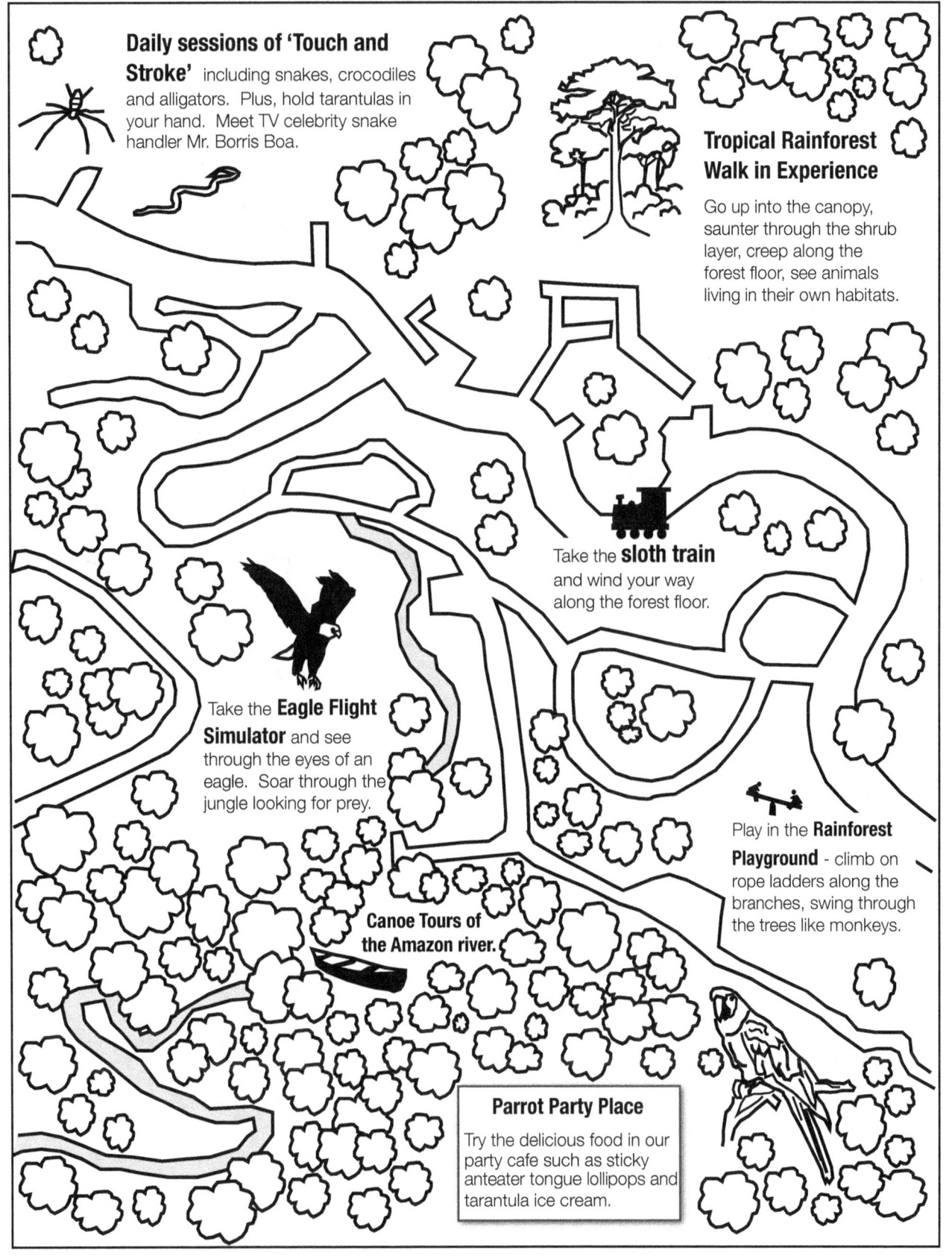

1. Recount a visit to a park called 'Rainforest World.'
(Introduction - what I saw - what I did - food I ate - conclusion)

2. Now, imagine that you are a bird at a wildlife park called 'Rainforest World.' Write about a day in your life.

You could write about your daily routine: when you are fed, what you are fed, what you do in the day, who are your feathered friends in the neighboring cages. Write about the funny humans who come and stare at you –what they say.

To do this task you will have to put yourself in the place of an animal. We say you must <u>empathize</u> with them. What would they say if they could speak? They must have many funny stories to tell.

Who am I?

What kind of bird am I?
Where do I come from?
What is my cage/aviary/enclosure like?

- I am a red Macaw with bright feathers.
- Rainforest Experience is my home.
- My cage has a net roof so I can't escape.
- Flying from branch to branch is my favorite activity.

My day:

It starts at...
First the keepers...
The visitors come at...
They look in my cage and say...
I spend the morning by...
In the afternoon...
The keeper feeds me at...
A crowd of people watch...
Next I...
At six the bell rings to say...
After the visitors leave I...

- Visitors say, "What a pretty boy. How are you today?" and expect me to repeat.
- I am fed nuts and fruit in a bowl.
- Visitors push tasty treats through my bars which I enjoy.
- More than this, I like to grab the treats from their hands with my beak and see them get scared that I will peck them.
- I sleep with my head under my wing.

What I think of Rainforest World

I like Rainforest World because...
but I would rather be...
The humans, who stare, are...
though they can be unkind when...
My keeper is...
In the park, my best friends are...
The other birds I talk to are...

- It is safe here. We are given food and we don't have to hunt ourselves.
- But, I get no time to myself. There are always big smiling faces peeping into my cage.
- Sometimes I feel like I want to peck them.
- My neighbors squawk all the time and get on my nerves.
- I like to dart and dive, squawk and peck, flutter and fly, quarrel and fight.
- They help us hatch our eggs and look after our babies.

Now imagine that you have talked to the animals at Rainforest World. Look at the list below and decide which animal said what.

Now imagine that you are an animal there. Write a diary entry about a day in your life. Write all your personal thoughts down as if you were that animal. Write some interesting details.

> I look cute and cuddly, but if you entered my cage I'd gobble you right up!
>
> Look at those stupid humans. Do they have nothing better to do with their time?
>
> Tap on my glass and I'll press my nose up against the glass to see who's disturbing my peace.
>
> I don't feel like being stared at by humans today, so I'm going to stay in my nesting box and hide.
>
> I just wish I could escape!
>
> What time is dinner, I'm starving? I hope it is better than yesterday's meal.
>
> I've heard that safari park down the road is really nice. Do you know the animals there are not locked in cages, but allowed to roam free? That's the life!

Plan and write your own story - 'ESCAPE' - Animals escape from Rainforest World.

Writing a story ASK:

WHICH ANIMALS ESCAPE?

WHERE DO THEY ESCAPE FROM?

WHEN DOES IT HAPPEN?

HOW DO THEY GET OUT? WHY?

WHAT ADVENTURES DO THEY HAVE?

ARE THEY RECAPTURED?

1) Get your reader's <u>attention</u>. Make the first line interesting.

2) You could try linking your last line with your opening line.

3) Make your reader want to read on.

4) Keep him or her interested.

5) Keep to your title. Make it exciting. Get into your plot quickly and have lots of actions and problems. Try making your story humorous, but not silly and far-fetched.

Paragraph 1:	Introduce the animal characters, setting and plot. Tell the reader how they escape.
Paragraph 2:	Develop the plot - exotic animals are on the run. Are they seen on the road or in the woods? Does something exciting happen?
Paragraph 3:	Wind up the story. Are the animals captured? How? By whom? Are they sent back to the zoo or do they get away?

Use good words from these groups. Can you fill in the missing ones?

ADJECTIVES	NOUNS	VERBS	ADVERBS
hungry	rabbit	ate	greedily
	sun	shone	brightly
busy	bees		
active	ants		
scuttling	spiders		
green	grass		
crackling	sound		
		twitching	nervously
pointed	ears	flopping	down
		looking	anxiously
sharp	teeth		
		hopping	madly
		disappeared	mysteriously
		yawning	sleepily
soft	rabbit	feels	naughty
		purring	softly
wise	owl	screeches	deafeningly
		growls	fiercely
		chewed up	completely
horrible	silence		
		going	smoothly
		wrapped	around
eventful	day		
favorite	food		

ADJECTIVES	NOUNS	VERBS	ADVERBS
faint	meow		
		growling	menacingly
		snarling	viciously
big	fight		
naughty	look		
deep	voice		
revolutionary	satellite		
		trudged	sadly
		squawked	loudly
		think	quietly
		walk	stealthily
		barked	loudly
warm	feeling		

Try using these writing techniques:

alliteration - repeats letters or sounds

        A cute cat crept into the cottage.

onomatopoeia

        The cat landed with a **thud**.

personification

        The cat watched as the moon moved slowly across the sky.

The **RIGHT WORDS** are IMPORTANT.
Use good words.

Don't use SAID, but instead use:

screamed   explained   cried   commented   exclaimed

uttered   shouted   whispered   argued   suggested

answered   replied

Instead of walked, use:

bounded   jumped   marched

Use good verbs with nouns (present and past). These verbs need helpful words like 'was'.

- *Auntie was dragging Monster the dog.*
- *Sam's cat was stalking the birds.*
- *The soccer player was dribbling the ball.*
- *The kittens were climbing the curtains.*
- *The toddler was spilling food.*
- *The ducks were gobbling up some bread.*
- *The cat was scratching the chair.*
- *The wind was banging the door backwards and forwards.*
- *The fox was chasing the cat.*
- *The ASPCA was rescuing the dog.*

Lastly, **check grammar.**
Does it sound correct when you read it back?

Check spelling.
Sound out words, using sounds or syllables.

Check punctuation. Use ? . , "..." ' ! : -

PLAYFUL AS A KITTEN
Simile

HIS EYES WERE AS WIDE AS SAUCERS.

Similes compare things using like or as.

IT WAS RAINING CATS AND DOGS.

Metaphors describe things as something else.

Use similes and metaphors.

Guinea Pig Education **can help you use punctuation** in *your* writing.

Let's get going!

First, don't forget to **write in sentences**. Use **capital letters** and **periods**.

Jules belongs to **S**ydney at 12 **O**live **G**rove, **R**ushford.

Now try this one:

lois and lulu belong to anya at 14 chesterfield gardens rushford

---

Use a **!**

That's exciting!
What a surprise!
Oh bother!

Use a **?**

What do guinea pigs eat?

Hold out a piece of vegetable. Will your guinea pig eat it?

Now try this one:

guinea pigs like to be stroked do they bite they are timid but rarely bite ouch

---

Do not forget to use "**.....**" when you use **direct speech**.

"Anya, what did you buy at the pet shop?" said Jules.
"I bought a cage, some straw, some hay, a bowl, a water bottle and some food for my new guinea pigs."

Use commas for **Lists**.

Use commas **before or after** a **phrase** or subordinate **clause** in a sentence.

Use commas **around a clause hidden** in the **middle of a complex sentence**.

Try these:

Lois is lively inquisitive and nosy

Guinea pigs can be chocolate black silver white and tortoise shell.

My guinea pig called Jules has long hair.

After cleaning the cage Anya put in some hay.

Try these: *(answers on next page)*

What is your guinea pig like anya

Lulu has a white coat, uneven colored spots and black ears she replied

After running in the grass Jules dozed in his hutch.

Guinea pigs in the wild live in a burrow.

Some guinea pigs with long hair have rosettes.

Let's remember **apostrophes**:

> The carrot belonging to Jules is **Jules's carrot.**

> The hutch of Lois and Lulu is the **guinea pigs' hutch.**

Plus, remember apostrophes for shortened words.

> They are gorgeous.
> **They're** gorgeous.

Try these:

> The guinea pig belongs to Kate.
>
> The hutch of the rabbits George and Ginger.
>
> Isnt he sweet.

Finally, you can use a **colon** in a list.

> Jess had five smart guinea pigs: a short haired coat, a long coarse coat, a deep shining coat, a smooth coat and one with rosettes and twirls.

Or you can use a **semicolon** to separate two similar ideas in a list.

> Guinea pigs are sociable; they like company.

Try this:
> The male guinea pig is a boar the female is a sow.

Make a sentence with a :
Make a sentence with a ;

For extra information you may need to use a **dash** for a longer pause.

> Dad bought Anya a guinea pig - it was so sweet.
>
> Jules nibbled his carrot loudly - crunch, crunch, crunch.

Or you could use **parentheses** for extra information.

> The guinea pigs (Lois and Lulu) scampered across the grass.

Try these:

> Anya fed her guinea pig he was hungry.
>
> The rabbits George and Ginger are great friends.

How did you do?

- Lois and Lulu belong to Anya at 14 Chesterfield Gardens, Rushford.
- Guinea pigs like to be stroked. Do they bite? They are timid but rarely bite. Ouch!
- Lois is lively, inquisitive and nosy.
- Guinea pigs can be chocolate, black, silver, white and tortoise shell.
- My guinea pig, called Jules, has long hair.
- After cleaning the cage, Anya put in some hay.
- "What is your guinea pig like, Anya?"
  "Lulu has a white coat, uneven colored spots and black ears," she replied.
- After running in the grass, Jules dozed in his hutch.
- Guinea pigs, in the wild, live in a burrow.
- Some guinea pigs, with long hair, have rosettes.
- Kate's guinea pig/ the rabbits' hutch/ Isn't he sweet.
- Anya fed her guinea pig - he was hungry.
- The rabbits (George and Ginger) are great friends.
- The male guinea pig is a boar; the female is a sow.

Aren't I sweet?

Of course!

Guinea Pig **Spelling** *Tips*

Guinea pig says, "Don't forget it is important to read through your writing, so you can spot any obvious mistakes. Here are a few basic spelling tips. Make sure you can spell all the words on these pages."

Tricky homophones

Homophones sound the same but are spelled differently.

I gave **two** carrots **to** Jules but he's getting **too** fat.

Our guinea pigs **are** cute.

They're over **there** by **their** hutch.

Difficult Endings

Some words have tricky endings.

The **latch** on Jules's **hutch** comes open. He gets out and eats a **patch** of grass by the **hedge**. I try to **catch** him but he **dodges** me and runs off.

When I **handle** my little piggy, I **cuddle** him.

Some words have spelling rules.

You double the final letter of a verb with a short sound.

I **hug** Jules.
I am **hugging** him.

I **pat** the rabbit.
I am **patting** him.

I **grab** him.
I am **grabbing** hold of him.

He **hops**.
He is **hopping**.

If the final letter is a consonant, just add the ending.

He **licks**.
He is **licking**.

He **fights**.
He is **fighting**.

I **hold** him.
I am **holding** him.

Drop the 'e' if you are adding an ending with a vowel.

I **love** my guinea pig.
I am **loving** him.

I **stroke** my guinea pig.
I am **stroking** him.

He is having an **adventure**.
He is **adventurous**.

Use the same rule for:

shine   shiny
noise   noisy

But, if the ending begins with a consonant you keep the 'e':

live   lively

love   lovely

lone   lonely

safe   safely

When you add an ending some words change the 'y' to an 'i':

My guinea pig is **happy**.
He is **happier**.
He is the **happiest**.

busy   busier   busiest
cry   cries   cried
piggy   piggies
carry   carries   carried

	Comparative	Superlative
He is fast.	faster	the fastest
He is fine.	finer	the finest
He is a beauty.	more beautiful	most beautiful

Use Sounds

ch, sh, wh, th, oo, ee, ar, or, ur, ir, er, e, ai, ay, oi, oy, oa, ow, ou, au, aw, ce, ci, cy, ge, gi, gy, short y, long y, magic e…

… to sound out 80% of words.

Use syllables to sound out hard words.

Eat **VEG ET ABLES**
Soft 'g' - ge, gi, gy.

are **COM FORT ABLE**

like **MIX TURE**

have an **AD VEN TURE**

SEV EN

PRECIOUS

CREATURE

Remember:

1. Sound hard words out using syllables.

2. Jot down words you find difficult. Learn them.

3. Use a dictionary or thesaurus.

Don't forget to keep your writing neat. Small letters should be the same height. There should be one little finger space between each word.

Make sure you can write this passage:

My guinea pigs feed on green leaves. They munch, crunch, scratch, scrunch in their hutch. Early in the morning it is necessary to feed them healthy food and fill up the water container. My noisy young pigs enjoy playing excitedly in their run on the lawn, where they are safe from danger.

Really tricky ones:

'i' before 'e' except after 'c' - when the sound is ee.

believe

fierce

field

conceited

Exceptions:

neighbor

Silent Letters:

Guinea Pigs:

gnaw

clim**b**

eat crum**b**s

are caut**i**ous

are ca**l**m

are **k**nowing

wrinkle up their noses

Tricky words:

Are you **tough enough** to keep a guinea pig?

They can't be **caught**.

They fill one with **laughter**.

They love to be **photographed**.

Guinea pig says, "Make lists of tricky words you find difficult from the groups of words."

The glossary

A starting point:	is something that gives you an idea to write a story.
The genre is:	the type of story you choose to write. It could be a traditional tale, that has a message that good overcomes evil, or a romance, horror, fantasy, mystery, realistic or adventure story.
Planning a story:	Structuring the story into three or more paragraphs – with a beginning, a middle and an ending.
Characters:	are people who feature in the story – we learn how they behave and about their feelings, motives, emotions and conflicts.
A setting:	is the place where the story takes place - creating a mood.
The Plot:	is a sequence of events that make up the story. Action in the story may be triggered by a conflict, complication, problem, or unexpected event that needs to be solved.
Suspense:	is built up to leave the reader guessing what will happen. Use: • short sentences for impact – 'Help!' • show the feelings of the characters – 'suddenly his heart missed a beat' – to build up a dramatic climax that leaves the reader on the edge of his chair wondering how it will end.
First person:	tells the story, using 'I' or 'we' – so the reader can imagine being the main character.
Second person:	uses 'you' and speaks directly to the reader or involves the reader.
Third person:	uses 'he,' 'she,' 'it,' 'they' to tell the story as a narrator, like a fly on the wall watching.
Atmosphere:	is the mood and feeling conjured up in the story.
Flashback:	if you start your story with action, you may include a few details about what went on before.
Ending or resolution:	may be happy, sad, moral (a lesson learned) or a cliffhanger - where the reader imagines his or her own ending.

Paragraphs:	start a new line (one finger space in for handwriting). Use a new paragraph if you change event, time or place.
Conjunctions:	are linking words that start paragraphs or join sentences. Examples are: as, since, because, but, if, then, so, as a result of, for instance, yet, after a while, suddenly.
Dialogue:	is what people say and can move the story on. Use correct punctuation – *Lilly said, "Is it hot in here?"* (direct speech); *Lilly said that it was hot in here.* (indirect or reported speech)
The opening:	is the first sentence of a story - fiction or narrative.
A topic sentence:	is the first sentence in a paragraph, which tells the reader what it will be about. Further sentences will develop the idea and explain it.
Describe:	is making a word picture.
Adjective and noun:	*shimmering sand* (describing word, naming word)
Verb and adverb:	*shouting noisily* (action word, describes action word)
Powerful verbs and adverbs:	Choosing key words – *'a voice sounded mysteriously,' 'he nodded his head anxiously.'*
Similes:	compare using as and like – *'as white as snow'*
Metaphors:	compare two similar things, but don't use like or as. *'The dog was a little monster.'*
Script:	tells a story through the characters' dialogue.
Writers' techniques	include: * repetition * rhetorical questions - questions that don't need an answer * personification - giving an object human qualities * onomatopoeia - words that sound like their name * alliteration - several words that start with the same letter
Fiction:	includes story and narrative.
Non-fiction:	includes information, diaries, leaflets, reports, recounts, descriptions.
Purpose:	why it is written – to inform, explain, describe, persuade, advise or argue.
Target audience:	are the people the article is written for – to instruct someone on how to use a ..., to explain how to get somewhere, to persuade or convince the reader to do something.